T0149255

How to Determine the
ENNEAGRAM
Personality Type of *Others*

JOSEN KALRA

BALBOA.
PRESS
A DIVISION OF HAY HOUSE

Balboa Press books may be ordered through booksellers or by contacting:

Balboa Press
A Division of Hay House
1663 Liberty Drive
Bloomington, IN 47403
www.balboapress.com
1 (877) 407-4847

Because of the dynamic nature of the Internet, any web addresses or
links contained in this book may have changed since publication and
may no longer be valid. The views expressed in this work are solely those
of the author and do not necessarily reflect the views of the publisher,
and the publisher hereby disclaims any responsibility for them.

The author of this book does not dispense medical advice or prescribe the use
of any technique as a form of treatment for physical, emotional, or medical
problems without the advice of a physician, either directly or indirectly. The
intent of the author is only to offer information of a general nature to help you
in your quest for emotional and spiritual well-being. In the event you use any
of the information in this book for yourself, which is your constitutional right,
the author and the publisher assume no responsibility for your actions.

Any people depicted in stock imagery provided by Thinkstock are models,
and such images are being used for illustrative purposes only.
Certain stock imagery © Thinkstock.

Print information available on the last page.

ISBN: 978-1-5043-8080-5 (sc)
ISBN: 978-1-5043-8081-2 (e)

Library of Congress Control Number: 2017907989

Balboa Press rev. date: 06/06/2017

To my mother, who has been amazing in my life.

CONTENTS

PREFACE

THE ENNEAGRAM IS A SYSTEM OF knowledge that describes nine types of personalities. I have been a student of the Enneagram since 2001. I follow the teachings of Helen Palmer and David Daniels. In the summer of 2001, I first attended their workshop and was amazed. How incredible were the panels of the types! The way Palmer and Daniels teach the Enneagram is to let the panels of types come out by asking questions of a group (the panel) of each type. They start with type Three, then Six, then Nine. Then, they follow with the inner triangle of the Enneagram—One, Four, Two, Eight, Five and Seven. They do two rounds of panels and ask questions that bring out the personality type of each number. By the end of the workshop, I was so impressed that they did not present the Enneagram in a lecture format. They did not tell us what each Enneagram type was all about. In fact, they did not in fact say anything at all about the personalities. Instead, they let the panels do all the work. The panels were like mirrors, reflecting the personalities of the nine types.

After the workshop, I had to re-assimilate my reality. I flew for two weeks with a consciousness expansion. My mind grew as I observed and started to determine the Enneagram

Personality Type of everyone I knew and everyone I came across. It was fun to type others, and I got quite good at it. I worked with Helen Palmer, and she was able to confirm that I was great at figuring out the different Enneagram types of others. At the second Enneagram workshop (a follow-up workshop) in the summer of 2002, I was shown something that was remarkable and surprising to me. Daniels and Palmer showed the class a movie with a woman as the main actress, and the purpose was for each Enneagram student to see if he or she could determine the Enneagram type of the main actress in the movie. Of the twenty-seven students at that workshop, only three students got the right answer. I was one of those who got it right. It taught me that most people have difficulty determining the type of others. That realization eventually led me to write this book. Typing other people isn't an easy thing to do. However, it is a very valuable skill if you can learn to do it. Determining the Enneagram type of others gives you an insight into their inner workings. It allows you to create a space for love, acceptance, and compassion for others because each type suffers and has uncontrollable inner compulsive behavior that we can forgive and accept. When one understands that the people in your life have behaviors that are compulsive but bother you, all you have to do is understand that they basically cannot stop that behavior because it is part of their Enneagram Personality Type. That leads to acceptance, love, and compassion. This is also true because you yourself have an Enneagram Personality Type that suffers as well and has its own inner compulsions. Understanding your and others' Enneagram Personality Types is valuable as a way of relating to others and is helpful in one's journey through life.

I have determined the Enneagram type of other people by watching for cues and characteristics of each type. I do this without doing a proper typing interview. I can do the interview, but doing an interview is not always possible. Observing the characteristics of type is another way of figuring out the type of the person you would like to understand better.

The Enneagram is a personality system that describes a large amount of our inner selves. When shown their types, people resonate and identify with them. I developed these characteristics about type myself and confirmed them with Palmer and Daniels, who readily agreed that these cues and characteristics are valid ways of determining the Enneagram type of others in your life.

The Enneagram is an excellent tool useful for understanding yourself and others. If you read the right books and develop your understanding of the Enneagram, you are doing something that brings more love and acceptance into your life. For me, after I typed my parents and sister, I quickly started to accept them more fully and forgave them for things that were simply a part of their personality types that may have rubbed me the wrong way. I used to feel annoyed at my mother, but after understanding that she is a Two, I accepted that much of what she is doing by making suggestions to me was simply her way of helping and loving me. My uncle is a worker to the core. As a Three, he thinks in terms of work and thrives when working in his chosen profession. Because he is a type Three, he focuses on how to perform. I accepted his heart as that of a person who needs work to feel validated. I came to love my parents and uncle more because of that acceptance.

Most books about the Enneagram discuss the substance of the types, detailing information that is useful in understanding type. Other books focus on how to determine your own Enneagram type—some even have a sample test that you can take to help you figure out which type you are. None of the books in publication focus on how to determine the Enneagram type of *other* people. Thus, I have set out to tackle that task of helping you figure out the type of anyone in your life. Discovering the Enneagram brings love and acceptance into our lives. It does this by helping you understand another person and their insides. Bringing out the personality type of others is one way to bond and nurture better relationships.

I am a type Five, subtype totems/social, on the Enneagram. I use my observations of different types to bring you this book. I hope it helps you find more love and acceptance in your life as well as some fun when it comes to figuring out the personality type of the people in your life.

INTRODUCTION

What Is the Enneagram?

THE ENNEAGRAM IS A DEEP SYSTEM of psychology that has been called a tool, a map, and a mirror. It is all three of these things. It is also known as a system of self-awareness.

The Enneagram was initially discovered by Sufi mystics and carried forward by a man named Gurdjieff. From there, it was developed as a system of psychology by others, such as Ichazo and Naranjo, both pioneering psychologists in their day. Palmer and Daniels attended the workshop run by Naranjo and fine-tuned and developed their own workshop with a profound understanding of the nine types of personalities. The system is now very modernized and can be seen as a sophisticated tool of understanding yourself and others.

As you become aware of the nine different types of personalities, you learn things that are powerful for your own self-growth and path in life. The Enneagram is a map because it can show you the way to greater self-awareness; greater self-improvement; and better, healthier psychology. It has been called a mirror because it reflects the self. In other words, the Enneagram describes your feelings and ways of relating to others and yourself.

Much of this description of our psychology is unconscious, subconscious, and to some extent, conscious. The trick for self-growth and self-awareness is to understand your type more consciously so that you can create a space for choice. If you become aware of your fixation of attention, for example, you are taking a step forward. The fixation of attention is a part of your Enneagram type. It means that your attention to your external world operates to pick up only certain information from your environment. As you become aware of your fixation of attention and how it operates, you are becoming aware of a subconscious process whereby your attention picks up certain information in your environment. If you observe your own attention moving in a certain limited way, then you can make a choice—whether to actually give that information meaning to you or to disregard it. This is not an easy thing to pick up. It takes practice and a very good observing ability; however, once accomplished, it can be a powerful way of understanding your way and others' ways of navigating their worlds. Knowing about the fixation of attention allows for the understanding that each type picks up only a certain amount of information from the "data stream of reality"—a Palmer description of the fixation of attention.

All nine types have their own particular fixations of attention, and each type picks up different information from what surrounds us. That information can be described, understood, and, most importantly, observed. You can make a more informed choice when you realize that your fixation is just a habit and a pattern of your attention but not something to necessarily or subconsciously listen to. Also, if you become aware of your passion, on the Enneagram, you can navigate that passion better. This passion is something that grips every type. It is an automatic response to an internal insecurity that is built into each type. Sometimes, it feels good to listen to your passion, and sometimes, it feels like a necessity. Sometimes, it feels as though you don't want to listen but are gripped into doing so anyway. For example, the passion of type Five has been called greed or avarice. I call it retreating. The Five, when presented with emotion from other people, needs to either retreat to his or her mind or literally physically move to a more solitary or isolated space in order to feel more comfortable and process that emotional information. If the Five does not become aware of his or her passion, he or she is operating on automatic. But awareness of the passion allows the thought of either, "I'm not leaving this group just because there is some emotion in my environment, and I'll stick it out," or "I can anticipate my need to retreat, so I'll prepare myself to do so." When you know your passion is going to kick in, you can choose how to navigate that compulsion. Also, even if you have no choice, knowing that you have a passion to retreat, for example, gives you healthier self-awareness. All parts of the Enneagram are this way. If you value self-awareness, you should study this system.

All major religions say to "know thyself". The Enneagram is a large system of knowledge and describes a lot of our inner behavior. It can be used to help you know yourself and others in your life. When you become aware of other people's personality types on the Enneagram, it becomes much easier to forgive those others you may have had conflicts with in the past. Much of people's behavior is automatic, done without being fully aware of what they are doing. When you understand your girlfriend better, or your cousin or coworker, you are able to accept that the person has a habit of acting a particular way.

For example, if you understand that type Five has a passion to retreat to the mind, you may try to have an intellectual conversation with that Five rather than a feeling one. You could share some knowledge with that person and watch the Five get more engaged. If you understand that the Five needs to retreat to his or her mind and has some unconscious fear of emotion, when he or she frowns at something, you can discern that that frown is not at you but at the emotion the person feels from you. Also, the Five may need to retreat to a private place rather than carry forward with the conversation—don't project reasons why the Five is leaving. It probably isn't because he or she is feeling something negative about you. Rather, it is about the need to be alone to process the conversation you just had.

The acceptance that the Enneagram creates is one of its greatest blessings. When that acceptance occurs, you may feel better, freer, more forgiving, and more able to grow. The acceptance that the Enneagram gives is greater the more you know about the Enneagram and the more you are able to successfully type others.

With acceptance comes love. Let's say you are trying to determine your husband's Enneagram type. You believe him to be a type Eight. He sometimes gets into fights with you, and you may feel badly about the fight. You come into the Enneagram material and realize that the fight is his way of being engaged with you; it is his way of lusting (his passion) and his way of feeling connected and more alive. He doesn't see the fight as a fight at all, but rather as a more assertive way of engaging with you, and it is not a reason not to feel love for you or a reason to break off the relationship. Instead, the fight becomes a source of communication and understanding, and you are able to love your husband more because you understand that the fight is just his way of relating to you. He may not even see the fight as a fight but rather as only an engaging conversation. I characterize the Eight's behavior as a fight because it can be perceived as such by others but not necessarily by the Eight. When the next fight comes, instead of wanting to stop the fight and have a more civil conversation, you engage the fight with your husband and watch how he responds in a positive way to the argument you are having.

The same is true of type Five—if your husband is a type Five and he spends a lot of time alone reading, don't interpret this to mean something about yourself or him. He isn't even being shy or wanting you to stay away. He is just alone because he feels more comfortable being alone. He needs to be alone to process information. He probably doesn't mind you coming into his space, because he loves you, but knowing that he has a passion to retreat can make you love him by accepting that he needs to be alone. That acceptance opens a space internally whereby you can have a better relationship with your Five husband. When you accept others' needs, you are showing them love. This can lead to better communication if you discuss the Enneagram types with someone else you care about. Your Five husband, knowing that he retreats and knowing that you are aware of his need to do so, feels given to and loved.

The statements below, in the chapters about the nine types, are meant to be identifiers. That means that the type of person you are trying to figure out should identify with the statements in this book. That is especially true for the bullet points in each chapter. Ask the prospective type if he or she identifies with these statements. Maybe he or she sometimes feels that way, might agree completely, or might simply not agree. The more self-aware a person is, the more likely he or she will be typed successfully by these identifiers. However, you may encounter a person who is not very self-aware and who agrees with many of the identifiers spanning multiple types. In this case, it becomes harder to type the person. But if you closely watch a person's behavior, you can learn to better observe and pick up cues and characteristics. Doing a typing interview will help you to compare the different possible types with the person you are interviewing. On balance and on average, the person you are trying to type will mostly identify with one of the nine types.

CHAPTER 1

LEARNING TO OBSERVE TO DETERMINE ENNEAGRAM TYPES

YOU CAN TAKE AN ENNEAGRAM TEST, but that may not be definitive. Further, some of the tests available are poor examples of how to accurately determine your type. In addition, none of these tests discusses ways for you to type another person without that second person taking the test. You can study the Enneagram, but learning to determine another person's Enneagram Personality Type requires observation and/or an interview as well as observation. Typing is critical in anyone's understanding of the Enneagram. It enables a whole host of ways of understanding yourself as well as other people you successfully type. What wouldn't be great about being able to walk into a group of people and simply identifying their types based on observation? After reading this book, you'll be more comfortable with your ability to type people simply through observation.

Observing means observing characteristics or cues about a person's personality. Use the identifiers in this book as well as the different understandings of Enneagram personalities embedded in the following chapters to determine the cues and characteristics of each type.

A tip on typing: There are three body-oriented types, One, Eight, and Nine. These types tend to be more in their bodies and feel their bodies more or use their bodies when interacting with others. Eights use their bodies to communicate even more than Ones or Nines.

There are three heart types—also known as feeling types—the Two, Three, and Four. There are three mental types: Five, Six, and Seven. Mental types use their minds more than other types. Sometimes, one can narrow down the person whose type you are trying to figure out into one of these three categories. If the person is outwardly emotional or feeling oriented, through the process of elimination, you might identify the person as a heart type. If they seem to use their minds to respond to questions, or you, for example, observe them being thoughtful and thinking their responses rather than responding with feelings, you can narrow down the possibilities to one of the mental types. Further, Eights are very physical people with a lot of their energy in their bodies. This is not a foolproof way of observing type. Anyone can use body language to communicate. But if you observe the physical way an Eight communicates, you can then do your typing interview by focusing on the type Eight questions and identifiers that are listed in this book. Again, with feeling types, narrowing down the possibilities means you can focus on asking questions of the Two, Three, or Four types. Another good way to narrow down type possibilities is to just ask the person you are interviewing whether he or she is a feeling type of person or a mental one. (Body types don't always identify as body types the way feeling and mental types identify as feeling and mental types.) That is based on my experience with Types.

For example, some people can be typed simply by how they use or don't use body language. Have a conversation with someone who has a large physical presence; he uses his arms to emphasize his points, and he comes across as a little bit intimidating and forceful. If you can observe a person using body language in strong ways as part of how they communicate with others, you're on track for determining the type of that person to be an Eight. Similarly, if the person you want to type seems quiet and hesitant to talk to others, perhaps sits in the corner, is a bit aloof, and responds with his head or his mind, then he may be a Five. Perhaps he nods a lot; perhaps you can tell that when he interacts with others that he is thoughtful when he responds. If you notice him bouncing a leg up and down repeatedly, that is a telltale signature body movement of a Five. No other types bounce their leg the way Fives do. Here we have two examples of how to observe and still successfully type. A note about observing to determine type—you aren't just looking at and listening for body language. There are other parts of the Enneagram (such as passions, fixations of attention, energy, energy structure, identification with language used by the person being typed by you, and core values of the different types) that you need to develop an ability to observe. So, a Five bounces his leg. That's his energy, located in the legs, that causes him to bounce. This is a trait of Fives. And the Eight comes across in a challenging confrontational manner; seeing the Eight's energy pick up when he uses his body language is yet another way of observing energy on the Enneagram. Each type has its own Enneagram energy structure, and that manifests in the way they communicate. This book will talk about how to observe in general, what to observe, and how to use those observations to determine type.

A second way to determine Enneagram type is to ask others questions about themselves. This doesn't have to be a test at all. It can simply be a friendly desire to understand the other person by asking some questions in order to bring out their personality type. This way of typing requires you to have decent Enneagram knowledge about each type. You can get that knowledge from other Enneagram books or workshops in addition to this book. You can also do a proper typing interview using the different identifiers or statements in this book. The chapters of the nine types of personalities in this book are designed for you to not only better understand the Enneagram in general but also to be used as a way of determining Enneagram personalities by asking questions. Use the identifiers in this book by turning them into questions to conduct a proper interview.

Observing and interviewing are the two primary ways of determining another person's Enneagram type. Observing can be seen as a skill learned through practice. You can learn to observe body language, facial expressions, energy pickups (meaning when a person's energy seems to increase and come out of them), energy structures (like the Five bouncing his leg), language used, and word choices coupled with energy pickups. Learning to observe what another person identifies with can be a difficult task and a bit confusing at first. Further, one can combine observations with questions.

For example, "Do you identify with x?" Therefore, we have making observations, doing a typing interview, and what I like most—observations coupled with questions.

When you ask people questions that are aimed at determining their Enneagram type, the best thing to do is to see if their answers to these questions are coming from the person's heart. If they start to get interested in the question or topic, if their energy picks up in excitement or interest, if they identify with the question or the answer, and if they agree with it in a way that reflects that their feelings go that way, you've made a great leap into figuring out their Enneagram type.

One exercise you can try is to ask questions of those whose Enneagram type you already know. Watch how their responses reveal their type. Learn to observe what they identify with. What questions are you asking that cause them to come out and become more interested in your conversation? Watching a person's energy pick up when asked certain questions can reveal which Enneagram Type they are. By practicing on someone whose Enneagram type you already know, you are learning what questions and answers resonate with that Type.

If a person agrees with having an inner critic, but does so in a lukewarm way, it is best to keep going through the other types before concluding with certainty that the person is a type One. It may be the case that a person being interviewed by you agrees with many parts of type One and type Two. The way to give more certainty to figuring out their type accurately is to watch and observe what kind of way they are responding to questions. Meaning, again, watching for excitement, or their feelings coming out on a particular topic or identifier. If their feelings come out more when asked a Two question/identifier, then they are more likely to be that type.

This is just an introduction to how you will learn to determine the type of people in your life. We'll go through each type and articulate ways of observing them. In the end, I hope you will use this book to determine the type of people in your life and/or anyone at all you encounter.

Doing a proper typing interview is the final way of figuring out someone's Enneagram type. The final chapter in this book discusses how to do that in a systematic way.

As I have said above, figuring out the Enneagram type of another person correctly and quite quickly creates a level of acceptance. If you have some knowledge of the Enneagram, then you immediately accept that their type is to do, feel, and act on certain characteristics of the type. For example, knowing that your friend is a type One immediately makes you accept that their criticism of themselves and others, their desire for correctness, to do the right thing, is part of who they are and not necessarily something that you should feel badly about or judge. That acceptance is the genius of the Enneagram. Understanding that type One has an inner critic that is often critical of themselves can help you to have compassion and empathy for type One. They suffer from their inner critic and respond or react to it more than other types do.

Another good point to raise about typing others is that

the grip that the Enneagram Personality Type has on us is strongest in our twenties and thirties. As we get older, this grip lessens even though we primarily identify with only one Enneagram type. When asking questions of prospective types, it can be helpful to ask them if a particular issue or subject was more prominent for them in their twenties and thirties.

CHAPTER 2

TYPE ONE

G O THROUGH THIS CHAPTER AND THE chapters that follow and turn the bullet point lists of identifiers into questions.

Ones are known as perfectionists. It makes sense since they are often trying to do the right thing. Again, the One may not see themselves as a perfectionist at first, but once you can see them being correct or correcting others and doing this as a way of relating to the world around them while at the same time noticing how frequently the One tries to fix the wrong in the environment, you can help that One understand themselves as a perfectionist.

+ It can be good to just ask the prospective types whether they see themselves as a perfectionist.

The One has a fixation of attention that looks for error as well as correctness or incorrectness in their external and internal environments. The One watches out for the opportunity to correct themselves or others. If you find a person correcting errors in their surroundings, that person could be a One. Determining Enneagram type is a bit like making an educated guess. It is not a science; rather, it is an art. See if you can figure out the fixation of attention for the One by watching what he or she pays attention to. If you can see errors in your own environment and then see if the prospective One corrects the error, you're probably going to see correctly that the person is type One.

- A great question to ask the One is if he or she experiences an inner critic frequently talking to them. All Ones have an internal critic telling them in their thoughts what should or shouldn't be done. They are critical people who think in terms of correctness. You might say that everyone has an internal critic, but for type Ones, this is something they strongly identify with. Everyone can think in terms of criticality or correctness, but the One does this as a way of relating to the world around them. Thus, Ones identify with their inner critic as being part of their internal selves more strongly than other types do.

A certain amount of the Enneagram involves unconscious behavior that someone may not be fully aware of. For example, the person who is a One but doesn't realize they have a fixation of attention that watches for errors or incorrectness is typical of that person before he or she comes into the Enneagram material. Once shown their fixation, they can develop an ability to observe their own fixation of attention. Asking the Ones if they pay attention to error in their environment may or may not bring out their type's energy or intelligence. Instead, showing the person their fixation of attention is to pay attention to error is a way to educate the person you want to type about his or her internal selves. If you can observe a One's fixation of attention, you can then bring it out of the One. Point it out right after the One corrects something. When it happens again, point it out again. The fixation of attention is a repeating pattern; it keeps happening and not infrequently. It happens throughout the day, each day, for that person's entire lifetime.

- Ones are judgmental and critical people. Ask if they identify with being this way.
- Ones experience themselves as good people, trying to do what is correct, just, or moral. This is another identifier for type One.

Their passion on the Enneagram is anger; it does not mean they are angry people or get angry frequently. What it means is that anger, often in subtle ways, comes out of them through their criticality and judgmental selves. A tinge of anger accompanies their critical statements. See if you can observe their anger when they get critical. Ones are sometimes a little bit angry; their anger leaks out of them. You aren't looking for an outburst of anger; rather, you're observing slight anger through criticality. This criticality can be towards themselves or others.

- If the One has an outburst of anger, the next internal step for the One is to judge that anger. Ask prospective Ones whether they judge themselves after getting it wrong (anger being a "wrong" emotion). Ask Ones whether they judge their anger after getting angry. This is an example of self-criticality.

+ Ones seek to improve the world in various ways; they are also called reformers. They try to reduce disorder in their environment. Ask if they do this. Something to note: many people might identify with the statement that they try to reduce disorder in their environment. A way to narrow it down to type One is to ask if they do this on a frequent basis and whether they feel part of their personality is to improve the world in various ways. Also, remember to ask if the person identifies as doing this more so in their twenties and thirties (when the grip of the Enneagram Personality Type is strongest).

+ Integrity, being good, and doing good are values that the One has. Ask them if these values resonate with them. Also, they have a self-image of being sensible, moderate, and objective. Ones reinforce their self-image by trying to live their lives in accordance with their conscience and reason. They are highly ethical and self-disciplined and possess a strong sense of purpose and conviction. Truthful and articulate, they teach by example, putting aside personal desires for the greater good. Ask the One if these statements resonate. If yes, you can conclude that they are likely to be type Ones.

+ Ones may sometimes feel they are wasting time if they are not improving themselves and their environment in some way.

- Ones have intuition regarding doing the right thing. They have an ability to know how to do the right thing, particularly regarding moral values.

- Ones frequently engage in self-criticism. They can be very sensitive to their inner critic, feeling as though they need to measure up to it.

- Ones care deeply about being good people and are moved into action by wanting to do something about the problems they see around them. This might manifest as wanting to save the environment, alleviate poverty, or do something for those less fortunate. Ones firmly believe they can make a difference.

Acceptance

Knowing that Ones have a serious inner critic can lead you to have more love, compassion, and acceptance of a type One. You know that they are suffering from their inner critic and basically just trying to do the right thing. Their point of view on the Enneagram is to be a perfectionist. If you see their perfectionist behavior as part of their way of relating to the world, you can navigate these people better. You can say to yourself that the criticism they make of others is coming from a desire to make improvements and make things better. You might also find compassion knowing that the One is hard on himself and suppresses his desire for pleasure by being critical of himself and others. You might also understand the passion of the One is anger, and if you notice his criticality coming with some anger directed at you, you can forgive that anger since you know is just part of the

One's personality structure. His passion makes him angry, and he expresses that anger through criticism or criticality. Ones are hard on themselves. Their inner critic makes it this way. Talk to the One about his inner critic and bring out his feelings and thoughts about his inner critic. You will open up to each other. You will develop love, acceptance, and forgiveness by just having an in-depth conversation about the One's inner critic.

CHAPTER 3

TYPE TWO

T YPE TWO IS THE GIVER. TYPE Two is a feeling-oriented
type, a heart type.

+ Ask the Two if he or she is a feeling-oriented person
as opposed to a mental one. The Two should respond
that they feel their way through life more than they
think their way through life.

If you can, narrow down the person you are typing into a
feeling-oriented type. From there, there are only three
possibilities remaining: Two, Three, or Four. Since Threes
suppress their feelings through doing and work and having a
successful image, they are less likely to identify as a feeling-
oriented type. Thus, using the following questions and
making certain observations, you can narrow down the
possibilities to a Two or a Four.

See if you can observe the prospective Two as someone who
is focusing on other people. Twos tend to think of others
before themselves. They "merge" and "become" as a fixation
of attention, and therefore merge with the feelings of others.
See if they are focusing their attention on other people's

needs. Ask them if they feel like they can feel the feelings of others inside themselves. This is not an easy thing to notice, but with repeated inner observations and practice inwardly observing, the Two can realize that their attention goes into other people's hearts often at the expense of their own feelings.

- Ask them whether they feel their way through life. Do you literally feel the road signs while driving? One Two told me she feels other people when engaging in conversation. My mother, a Two, once said that when I was a child, I fell from the top of a jungle-gym bar and landed on my back. She literally felt her own back hurt. How can that be? The Two sees things in a relational context and merges with others' feelings. That merging is what made my mother feel her own back hurt even though it was me who fell, not her.

- The Two has a hard time handling his or her own needs but is quite good at understanding the needs of others. Also, they may experience confusion in figuring out their own needs, but also an intuitive understanding of others' needs.

- Twos think in certain ways relating to their type. They feel pride in the importance of themselves in relationships ("They'd never make it without me") and pride in meeting the needs of others ("I don't need anyone, but they all need me"). Thus, ask the Two if they think these ways: Do you think that others would never make it without me or that others would not be successful without me? Their sense of self-worth comes from the approval of others and their belief that they are indispensable to others.

Twos have a fixation of attention that alters themselves in order to meet the needs of others. This can lead to intuition or empathy about others and can lead to a twisting of themselves into the wishes of others to assure love and positive attention.

+ Further, Twos believe themselves to be great at bargain hunting and negotiating over a purchase. My mother, a Two, is always on the lookout for a bargain or a discount. It is a telltale sign of the Two. Thus, try asking the potential Two whether they are frequently or always on the lookout for a good deal, whether they buy things by negotiating over their price, and whether they feel they are good at bargaining and bargain hunting. See if their energy picks up when answering this question. Do they laugh and agree? Do they smile and does their interest grow?

+ Twos value community and think in terms of using and being a part of community. That is a value they have that you can ask them about. Also, they see people as resources and think in those terms. Again, see if the Two identifies with and has their energy pick up or if their heart feelings come out when asked about community and people as resources.

Twos are called the helper or giver because they are genuinely helpful to others or possibly invested in seeing themselves as helpful. The love and concern they feel for others and the genuine good they do makes Twos feel worthwhile.

See if you can observe a Two parent in their parenting role. Twos embody the perfect parent. They see their child as they are, understands them with immense compassion, helps and encourages with infinite patience, and is always willing to lend a hand. They can often have intuition on their children's needs, making them superb parents.

- Twos have a self-image of being loving and selfless—selfless because they are putting other people in front of themselves and loving because they are often giving and helping others.
- Twos sometimes feel tired from overdoing other people's needs. They may also feel underappreciated for the work they do for others.
- Twos are sincerely encouraging and extremely appreciative of the talents and strengths they find in others.
- On a more negative side, you might ask, "Do you feel taken advantage of by others to whom you have supported or helped and not gotten positive or grateful responses from?" The Two will probably answer this question in the affirmative.
- In general, the Two is a giving type of person and will identify as such.

Acceptance

The Two has a fixation of attention that transforms themselves into the feelings of others. That is hard to observe. However, knowing that they become and merge and then adopt a stance of being the helper can be something to look out for and develop an ability to observe over time. The Two seeks out positive attention and approval from others. They focus on your needs first. If you know the person you are interacting with to be a type Two, you can accept that they are looking for love and positive attention by focusing on other people's needs. I used to be angry at my mother for always telling me what I needed to do. But once I understood her to be doing that automatically and from a subconscious desire to be loved and given back to, I felt more acceptance and love for her. What was nagging me from her became, "Okay, Mom is just trying to help me." That internal shift in myself makes me nod and smile at my mother, who is truly a great helper and has been that way throughout my life.

Also, the Two looks to use community and others as resources. If the Two you are interacting with wants to use others and for some reason you do not want to, you can at least understand that this is her natural way of thinking about the world and how to resolve problems. Your judging self will accept rather than get angry or be critical of the desire to seek help from powerful people when you feel differently about engaging with that powerful person that the Two wants to use as a resource.

A good way of accepting a type Two is to give them positive attention. This means telling them that you appreciate their help, be gentle with criticism, and to take an interest in their problems since they sometimes have trouble figuring out their own needs. Twos thrive on positive attention and seek it out in order to feel loved and validated. Giving them positive attention will create a loving interaction between yourself and the Two you're interacting with. On the other hand, Twos shun negative attention. Knowing this, it is best to keep giving them positive attention. Otherwise, they will have a hard time dealing with the negative side of a person's feelings if directed toward the Two.

CHAPTER 4

TYPE THREE

TYPE THREE IS CALLED THE PERFORMER or the achiever. This is because he or she thrives when performing and has a focus of attention that involves how to perform well. Performance is part of how Threes see work, and work is what Threes thrive on. Often, this is at the workplace but can also be even when doing any kind of work at home. Work doesn't necessarily mean only their job or career, but any work being done such as gardening or fixing a broken door knob. The Three thrives on work, needs work to feel fulfilled, and doesn't like sitting idle. Contrary to Nines who like to just be, the Three likes to work at it—to keep working and learn through doing. The Three is an image type. They adjust their image with other people so as to look and be successful with others. Success is critical to the Three, and achieving through doing is a part of their modus operandi. Threes identify with accomplishment and success. One Three said, "My identity is based on what I do." They seek approval and acceptance based on performance. They feel a constant pressure to perform.

My uncle, a Three, often gives me advice to just keep working at it. His attitude is that you can learn through doing and accomplish things by working at it.

The United States is a Three culture. We focus on work, image, and productivity and value those qualities. The worldview of the United States and the Three are aligned, further justifying and supporting the Three's worldview.

- The Three core value is work and/or achievement. They need and focus on work and accomplishments as a way of life. They cannot sit idle and always are on the lookout for work to do.
- Ask the Three if they adjust to others. Do they shift their presentation or image to look good in front of others? That is the passion of the Three—image or deceit. It has nothing to say about the Three being deceitful, and the shifting of their image may or may not be so conscious; it is their passion to adjust their image so as to look successful. The Three sometimes finds himself, subconsciously at times, changing their image in a way that suppresses their true feelings. This is because they feel the need to look good in front of others, even if they might be feeling angry, negative, or different from the impression they are giving off. That is why the passion is called deceit. Their outward image does not always reflect their true self.
- The Three is a feeling-oriented type but isn't as in touch with his feelings as a Two or a Four. Threes would rather do than feel.
- The Three focuses on tasks, goals, and recognition. This is part of a fixation of attention to focus on these areas.

+ The Three worldview is that life is about appearing successful. Ask the Three whether this resonates with how they think and feel about life. Also, Threes tend to believe they are their accomplishments and that they can adapt themselves to match the circumstances and that everyone wants to be known as a winner.

As noted above, Threes present an image that is adjusted to gain approval. This intuitive adjustment often happens even to the point of believing that the image is one's true self. If probed into, this adjustment can be a source of suffering where there is confusion between their image and their true self. Sometimes, when coming into the Enneagram material, a Three has to reassess his image. They have a conflict internally between their truthful feelings and the need to look good in the eyes of others. A Three believes that his or her image can help achieve his or her objective.

+ You can ask Threes if they think this way, that their image is part of how they succeed and that it helps them achieve.
+ Threes come across as highly focused achievers. The Three's self-esteem is riding on a win. Personal values and security depend on how much they can get done.
+ Threes measure their value in terms of what impresses others. They believe they have little value aside from what they do. They find identity through a task.
+ Threes feel alive in the midst of activity and become adept at sensing the energy requirements of different jobs.

+ Threes are wedded to their work. They are often seen as workaholics.

+ Question for Three: Would you rather sit idle and relax or keep occupied and busy when on vacation? Threes will answer that they would rather keep busy.

+ Threes have a desire for lifelong learning and an ability to find interesting things to do. Threes possess a natural ability to present themselves and their projects in an effective way. There is an interest in supporting social programs that help people rise materially by their own efforts and in developing future leadership.

+ Adaptable, excelling, driven, and image-conscious all describe the Three.

+ People often look up to the Three because of their graciousness and personal accomplishments. Ask prospective Threes whether they feel looked up to based on their accomplishments.

+ Threes enjoy motivating others to greater personal achievements than others thought they were capable of. My uncle often does this with me. He encourages and tries to motivate me to overcome my hurdles in life and be successful. He finds ways for me to excel in whatever I might be interested in.

+ Threes believe in developing their talents and capacities.

+ Threes believe in the statement, "If I work hard, I know I can do it."

+ Threes can equate their own personal value with their level of success. Some Threes are intensely interested in success and are determined to distinguish themselves through professional achievement and by possessing a variety of status symbols. Status symbols might include such things as owning a Mercedes or being the elected head of their department at work.

+ Threes pay attention to performance in all senses of the word—professional, physical, academic, and social. Threes present themselves to others as someone who has it all together, with a cool, effortless mastery. Their fixation of attention gravitates toward performing. That means that they will pay attention to how they themselves will, should, or did perform as well as how others perform. Ask the Three if they think this way and observe this way.

Threes are good communicators and promoters, and they know how to present something in a way that is attractive, appealing, and inspiring. At the very least, they focus on this and try to figure out the best way to communicate. My uncle often tells me how much he admires President Obama's speaking ability. He watches how the former president communicates, and my uncle tries to communicate well himself as a way of being successful.

Acceptance

When presented with retirement, my uncle had to find another job rather than retire. He is a type Three. My aunt wanted to travel, but my uncle needed work. That conflict has presented itself before between them. But after my aunt understood type Three to be compulsive workers and that they need to stay busy, her level of acceptance for him grew.

Threes also bond when working with someone. I know my uncle bonds with me when we do things like put a desk together for my new room or work on fixing something in the house. That bonding experience makes my uncle love me more. He remembers that experience when he thinks about his own love for me.

They are known as workaholics, and once accepted as needing work, having a hard time being idle, and encouraging others to just work at it, one can generate love through that acceptance like it has created love between my uncle and I. I know him to be compulsive in needing work and that he thinks in terms of work. He learns by doing and thrives on performing. Just knowing that about him gives me more love and acceptance of him. When Threes encounter a physical limitation that prevents them from performing, perhaps a bad back or a broken leg, they suffer much more because they cannot work or perform. Knowing that my uncle's knee injury may have prevented him from performing gave me more compassion for him. I understood he wasn't just suffering from a bad knee but rather from his own inability to perform. This can even lead to a depressed state in the Three. Thus, one can have more love, compassion, and acceptance for a Three in your life by understanding how an injury is preventing the Three from being himself, from not being able to work, or perform as well as his expectations.

Threes thrive on performing and accomplishing; thus, it is great to love the Three by telling him you are proud of his accomplishments. Threes have a hard time putting up with inefficiency and incompetence. For example, a supervisor trying to accomplish tasks but runs into staff who are not doing their job properly can be very frustrating to the Three. You can relate to the Three by lamenting the staff's incompetence and encouraging him to stick it through and understand that not everyone is as focused on performing well as he is.

CHAPTER 5

TYPE FOUR

FOURS ARE CALLED INDIVIDUALISTS. THEY ARE very much individuals and see themselves as unique people. They stand out from others with their feelings and are emotive and dramatic. Type Four is a deep-feeling type. See if you can observe the Four as he expresses feelings and operates from his heart. Fours have a natural ability to feel people, issues, and subjects deeply. Ask the Four if they feel deep feelings often. The Four is a dramatic type of person. That is, they act out in dramatic fashion their needs and feelings. See if you can observe a Four being dramatic in behavior. They might be called drama queens for their way of dramatizing life. One friend of mine in law school, a Four, used to come out in support of ending the war on drugs and used to bring up this issue that she was passionate about—stopping overly harsh sentencing laws for first-time drug offenders. The class was about criminal procedure, but the war on drugs was not being discussed. It was a basically irrelevant question to bring up and was out of context, as the professor noted back to her. However, she continued to be dramatic and emotive when it came to the issue. She was standing out in class by acting out her heart. She had a flamboyant way of speaking up that caused others to snicker at her, but I was able to appreciate her for being outspoken and even dramatic about the issue she cared about so much. Better not to judge the drama of the Four and instead accept it as part of the personality type.

+ The Four searches for authentic connections to others. Fours value authenticity. Ask the Four if they value authenticity, and they will say yes. Bring them out by following them when they answer that question: "Do you seek genuine and authentic connection to others as part of your way of relating to others?" You may also be able to observe when a Four seeks authentic connection to others. They bond that way.

Fours have a passion on the Enneagram system called envy. This means that they gravitate toward people who are generating heart energy. For example, if someone is talking with their hearts, emphasizing certain points, and they are coming out of their shell with something they are very enthusiastic about, that causes the Four to want to be a part of that heart energy. Their passion will kick in to make them want to bond with the person expressing themselves with heart energy. See if you can observe this happening and watch for it. Envy does not mean jealousy; it is just a passion of the Four to bond with and want to bond with those whose hearts are coming out.

+ Fours can at times feel a deep lack of self-worth and a need for constant comparison with others. There is a sense that mine isn't as good. The grass is always greener on the other side of the fence. Someone else always has it better, seems to be happier, or seems to have the perfect relationship. One Four remarked that when she sees couples together, they always look as though they are more loving together and are doing better than the relationship she is in. It is like wanting something that isn't quite within reach.

+ The Four strives and often desires something that they cannot have and aggrandizes the unattainable. Fours experience a feeling of great longing. Ask the Four if this is a part of their life. This is a very unique quality of the Four—a constant longing for something unattainable. Once attained, it no longer seems so good, and the need for longing for a distant lover re-emerges. This is another way their passion, envy, manifests.

Fours are very emotive people. They express feelings with emphasis. See if you can observe the way the Four expresses their feelings. They have a flair for the dramatic that can also be observed with practice. They express a wide range of feelings.

+ They see themselves as unique, special, and different. Something sets them apart. They feel something about themselves that makes them not fit in with other people. This becomes the Four identity.

+ Fours will identify with the statement: "Not I think therefore I am, but rather, I feel therefore I am. My feelings come first."

+ Fours are dramatic, temperamental, and self-absorbed as well as sensitive to feelings.

They experience longing for someone to rescue them and sweep them away from their dreary mess.

+ They feel that finding themselves and being true to their emotional needs have been extremely important motivations for them.
+ They are aware of their own intuitions, feel things deeply, and can be very intuitive.
+ They maintain identity by seeing themselves as fundamentally different from others.
+ They are overly or acutely aware of and focused on their personal differences and deficiencies.
+ Fours feel like they are missing something in themselves, although they may have difficulty identifying what that something is.
+ They experience a desire to deeply connect with others who understand them and their feelings.
+ They feel like an individualist. Everything must be done on her or his own, in his or her own way and on his or her own terms.
+ They try to be true to themselves, and this is very important to them.
+ Fours have difficulty learning to let go of feelings from the past and a tendency to nurse wounds and hold on to negative feelings about those who have hurt them. They can become very attached to longing and disappointment.

Fours can live in their imaginations. Fours fantasize about people, events, and scenarios that stir up emotions they feel reflect their identity. They can find themselves fantasizing especially about potential romance, sexual encounters, or becoming an idealized self.

- Fours feel a degree of loneliness, an intense longing to be included, and envy of those who are included.
- To the Four, others seem to have it altogether. They have self-esteem, know how to present themselves, and go after what they want in life. Others seem to be spontaneous, happy, unself-conscious, and lively, all the things that Fours feel they are not.
- They can find themselves dwelling on unpleasant moods, wallowing in feelings. They can be overly attached to a mood of melancholy.
- Even when a Four has attained success, he or she still focuses on the lost love, the unavailable love, a future love, and a picture that only love can bring. They have a belief that their authentic self will be reawakened by love.
- Fours have a sensitivity to other people's emotionality and pain as well as an ability to support others in crisis. Fours are particularly suited to working with people going through crisis or grief. They have unusual stamina for helping others go through intense emotional episodes and are willing to stick with a friend through long periods of recovery. They say that if something dramatic, dangerous, or deeply disturbing happens, the Four finds himself immediately present.
- As deep feelers, Fours appreciate the deeper things in life—birth, death, beauty, love, and authentic connection to others. They search for depth of meaning.

- Fours focus of attention goes to the past, to the future, to the absent, to the hard to get. There is a preoccupation with that which is missing, such as the absent friend at the dinner party or the missed connections in an intimate talk.

- Fours can take on other people's emotions and can match the feeling tone of other people as a way of staying connected to them. They are very intuitive with their deep feelings. They also have an ability to pick up the feelings of others and can thereby empathize with others.

- They are drawn to the intensity in others. This is another way of seeing their passion—envy.

- Fours can exert a great deal of time and energy trying to obtain something appealing only to find fault when it comes within reach.

The above statements are identifiers. As in each chapter about each type, you can ask potential Fours about these statements and ask and observe whether they actually do identify with them.

Acceptance

One way of accepting a Four is to bond with them over something deep—may it be a beautiful painting, some powerful music that resonates with both of you, or even the Enneagram itself. This is loving the Four—to pay attention to the deeper more authentic aspects of life.

Another way of finding acceptance is to accept the drama that Fours exude. Their dramatic expressiveness is part of their hearts; it is not something to criticize, laugh at, or judge. Rather, it is just part of the way they are.

Further, you can help a Four by showing them that what they already have is good enough. Knowing that they have an internal habit of longing for what is missing and thereby undercutting what they already have and seeing what they already have as not good enough gives rise to not appreciating life for what it has already given us. If the Four is talking about a long-lost love or wishing to have the ideal romantic relationship, you might accept that as part of their personality type and not get annoyed at their insistence that they have something missing in their life. Also, acceptance and compassion are created when we understand that Fours wallow in melancholy and sometimes depression. The therapist dealing with a Four client can benefit from this understanding and acceptance of Four and help that Four learn to recognize these internal patterns. Maybe the Four is again wallowing in negative or depressing feelings and the therapist can try to help them get out of darker places that the Four experiences.

Compassion arises when we understand that the Four experiences dark moods of emotion, despair, or depression. The Four wallows in these deeper feelings much to their own detriment. They also feel as if nobody understands them and that they are unique and different. Just understanding that the Four suffers these ways gives rise to a compassionate attitude that one can take toward them. Also, understanding that type Four is a personality type gives rise to self-acceptance of these issues just by having a Four come into the Enneagram material.

CHAPTER 6

TYPE FIVE

FIVES ARE CALLED OBSERVERS. THEY OBSERVE and detach to their minds rather than participate with feelings and emotions. Fives are the intensely cerebral type, secretive and isolated. See if you can observe them as cerebral people. Do they seem mentally driven and oriented?

+ Fives have an internal drive of wanting to know.

They seek knowledge and have a desire to master the material. When studying, for example, a way of learning is to read the book to the point where they have mastered the subject. Then and only then does the Five come out of his or her shell to participate in the class. Mastery of a subject gives Fives security and confidence. This is as opposed to discussing the subject with the professor. Fives would often feel more comfortable reading the book before asking questions of their professor—unlike other types of people who might prefer to have a conversation to learn the material.

+ Fives have a love for knowledge. A good question to ask them would be whether they have a few books always by their bedside or what are they reading these days; they are voracious collectors of knowledge and thrive on collecting it.

Fives are very mental people who use their minds to navigate everything in their life. They respond to questions about what they know and bond over mental subjects. They avoid expressing feelings because feelings are hard to understand and come and go quickly.

See if you can observe whether the prospective Five is responding with thoughts or feelings. Can you observe his head moving in response to questions rather than his arms, whether he uses his mind to respond, whether his attention goes to his mind, or whether he responds by expressing thoughts rather than feelings? Going to the mind means bringing his or her attention to their minds for the purpose of thinking rather than simply responding to something with a feeling or emotion as their way of interacting. This understanding of the Enneagram isn't written in other Enneagram books. No other books teach you to pay attention to energy, attentional patterns (such as the Five detaching from his heart and going to his mind when responding to your questions), and responses that the tested person identifies with as part of himself. A good follow-up question in general would be to ask if the person you are trying to type resonates and identifies with what he just said. For example, after the Five says privacy is very important to him, you might ask in what way privacy plays a role in his life and in what way does he identify as a private person? Using the term "identify" helps you to understand what the recipient's type may be since the Enneagram is a system of understanding what the different nine types identify with internally. It is not an external system of psychology. As Palmer and Daniels say, "It's an inside job." We're finding out about the insides of people. It is not whether they like tennis or basketball but whether they have strong feelings about privacy or fairness, for example (Five and Eight core values).

+ Five core values are privacy and perhaps efficiency. "What does the word privacy mean to you?" is a good question to ask. All responses to this question cannot be listed. We don't know how the Five will respond to your questions. However, listening to him talk about privacy and listening well and observing his responses can help determine whether this person is a Five or something else.

+ If his energy, previously reserved, quiet and aloof, picks up and he becomes more animated when discussing privacy, you can conclude he is a Five. See if you can observe whether the prospective Five seems to identify with a question, statement, or topic like privacy.

+ All Fives have a review set up in their memories. They will often review (like remembering) moments of the day or recent past in their memories, especially when an outburst of emotion happens during the day. As a child, as a type Five myself, I would often sit in bed before falling asleep and review the day's emotional moments. Ask the Five if he or she reviews emotion-filled moments of the day right after they happen or before falling asleep at night. Since no other type has this sort of review, if the prospective Five says yes to this, then that is a quick and correct

> way of typing them as a Five. The review aspect of a
> Five is a telltale sign unique to Fives.
>
> + Another question to ask Fives is whether they feel
>   as though they have to think their feelings. Fives are
>   notoriously unaware of their feelings; they have an
>   attentional habit of going to their mind to retreat
>   from feelings. I can tell you from the Five perspective
>   that I have to figure out my feelings by thinking
>   about them rather than just knowing them or being
>   able to easily express them.

Further, the passion of the Five is retreat (also called greed
or avarice, but I call it retreat). Retreat means retreating both
to the mind to avoid feeling as well as literally physically
retreating from a group of people, so as to feel more
comfortable feeling his or her own emotions. The retreat to
an alone space feels like relief to the Five, who then probably
reviews the moments of emotion he just experienced when
in the group or with another person.

Fives have an energy structure that involves their legs. If you
see someone bouncing their leg, they are probably a Five.
The Five bounces his or her leg when stimulated in some
capacity. Bouncing it up and down, either leg, is a telltale sign
that that person is a Five. Their energy is just structured to
bounce that way. It might seem like a strange way to identify
a personality type, but the Five truly does have this kind
of internal energy structure that causes him to use his legs
this way.

> + The Five also has a character trait of being calm in
>   a crisis. Ask the potential Five if they resonate with

the idea of calmly handling a crisis situation. Has that happened to them before?

Fives can also be seen as or identify with being minimalists. They tend to try to make as much as possible out of as little as possible. They use fewer resources, do things efficiently, and try not to have as many possessions as other people might want. The term "minimalist" might resonate with a potential Five. In Nines, we see a materialistic streak. In Fives, we see an anti-materialistic streak. The Five seeks to avoid collecting things and doesn't want to clutter his or her environment with too much stuff.

+ Ask the Five if he tries to do with less. Ask him if he can see himself as a minimalist. "Does it feel good to be a minimalist?" is a potential follow-up question. The Five is not interested in collecting material possessions and status. Unlike the Three who wants the Mercedes for status, the Five may choose a more practical car and save some money at the same time.

A Five can often come across as sweet and thoughtful.

+ Fives think deeply. They are capable of generating deep thoughts on any topic.
+ Fives rarely exhibit emotion. They don't get emotional easily and tend to avoid expressing their feelings in an emotional manner. They have an internal desire to stay away from emotional expression. They are averse to emotionalism.

Acceptance

Fives have difficulty understanding their own feelings and the feelings of others. They live in their minds. This makes it especially difficult to relate to a Five, who might be quiet and aloof. Acceptance that Fives are not in touch with their feelings means you are less concerned with them expressing their feelings. A level of compassion can also develop when you realize that Fives suffer from not be able to understand their own feelings.

Fives are the loners of the Enneagram. They like and prefer to be alone much more than other types. When you understand Fives, you can accept them for being private individuals. They don't share their feelings mostly because they are not in touch with them. Knowing that Fives need to retreat to private spaces can allow for more acceptance in a relationship with a Five. They are not dismissing you when they feel a need to retreat; rather, they are processing information more easily when alone or when going to their minds to think about something. Further, a Five might reject having too much stuff; understanding that the Five doesn't want to collect things because it makes them feel somehow imposed upon can lead to a conversation about whether you truly need to make that purchase of something like more clothing, a third car, or anything that might seem unnecessary to the Five.

Some Fives have told me they don't like going to weddings. Another type's position might be that weddings are fun. But the Five knows that there will be a lot of people expressing emotion at a wedding and therefore shun going to such parties. The Five does not want to feel pressured to be around others when they know it will be difficult or uncomfortable for them. Recognizing this, one can accept that the Five has a hard time around people and feels that need to be alone rather than engage with others' feelings.

You can bond with a Five by being intellectual, mental, or discussing something they've been reading.

Fives rarely engage emotion. This can be a troublesome point in a relationship with a Five. There are still things that the Five will get excited and animated about, such as something they have been reading or studying. Knowing that the Five is rarely emotional leads to an acceptance of the Five that way—that is, one accepts them and has compassion for them in regard to the Five not being naturally able to express emotion.

CHAPTER 7

TYPE SIX

T HE SIX SEES BOTH SIDES OF the situation, the good and the bad. Called devil's advocates, they make good attorneys who can articulate both sides of an issue.

+ Ask prospective Sixes whether they identify as having a good and bad side to them—the devil on one side and the angel on another. Ask them if they ever feel as though they internally perform the devil's advocate position when analyzing an issue. The subject presents itself, then a "yes, but …" question emerges, and then "on the other hand," and the subject is analyzed.

Six is a mental type on the Enneagram. The Six has a doubting mind. This comes clear in meditation practice. When we observe our thoughts come and go in meditation, the Six has doubts about whatever comes up. Doubting mind dogs the Six. They are plagued by doubts. Doubt is what they do.

+ Ask prospective Sixes whether they have a doubting mind, and they will respond in the affirmative.

+ Sixes also have a certain relationship to authority. They may gravitate toward authority or feel contrary to authority. Sometimes, they feel like rebels against authority. Other times, they feel appreciative of authority such as appreciating police officers for the work they do as authorities themselves. They can be attracted to authority but are distrustful of it at the same time. In general, Sixes tend to be mistrustful of authority until they are reassured that the authority is benevolent and knows what he is talking about. Once Sixes have found a good authority, however, they strongly identify with it and internalize its values and teachings.

+ Ask the Six about authority and watch to see if the response and language used in their response is something they identify with, whether their energy picks up, and whether their feelings and heart pick up the issue of authorities and relating to authorities.

+ Sixes core value is trust. They find it hard to trust others and at the same time value trust in a relationship very highly. Their doubting mind sometimes causes them to mistrust others.

+ Ask the Sixes about trust and ask them if that is an issue they feel they grapple with. Also, the Sixes, because they doubt and lack trust in others, tend to crave reassurance. Ask them if they crave reassurance and again pay attention to how they respond. If their head bobs up and down and they seem to respond to this question with their hearts, then you've pinned them down as being a Six.

The Six worldview is that the world is a dangerous place where you have to expect the unexpected. If you plan for the worst, you will keep yourself safe. Don't trust anyone. Instead, take nothing at face value and be ready for the worst. Sixes make good policy makers because they see the pitfalls or dangers of any situation. They are great planners and focus on being prepared for any situation.

+ Ask the Six if they plan things out to avoid experiencing a dangerous or worst-case scenario type of situation.

Anxiety is something Sixes wrestle with often. This is driven by their doubting minds and passion of fear. Their passion doesn't always manifest as being afraid of something, but rather, it comes up as anxiety, doubt, mistrust, and worry.

+ Sixes are the committed, security-oriented types; they can be engaging, responsible, anxious, and suspicious.
+ Sixes can lack confidence in their own minds and judgments. That causes them to seek out security through others.

Sixes are always aware of their anxieties and are always looking for ways to construct social security bulwarks against them. If Sixes feel that they have sufficient backup, they can move forward with some degree of confidence. But if that crumbles, they become anxious and self-doubting. A good Six question is "When will I know if I have enough security?" "What is security?" would be a deep thought for a Six. Because Sixes have serious doubts about themselves and the world, they start to look for a sure thing that will guarantee their security—anything from a marriage to a job to a belief system to a network of friends to a self-help book. Most Sixes have more than one sure thing—just in case. They are the type that believes in saving for a rainy day and investing for the future and being loyal to a company in order to ensure their pension.

Sixes seek reassurance and guidance in procedures, rules, authorities, and philosophies.

- Sixes can be cynical at times.
- Sixes feel that life is fraught with dangers and uncertainties so it must be approached with caution and limited expectations.
- Doubt, questioning, believing, searching, skepticism, and resistance are always part of the picture.

Sixes can find freedom through structure. Many Sixes find a great deal of flexibility and creativity within the security of known boundaries. When things have a natural order, Sixes are content to work within it. Sixes feel safer when they have some sense of what to expect, so they typically dislike sudden changes. Having a certain amount of dependable predictability is comforting to their anxious minds.

Sixes have an extraordinary sensitivity to danger signals. While this kind of awareness can be an asset and help a Six, many Sixes remain hyper alert and hyper vigilant even when no danger is present. They can never relax or feel safe. The Six has eyes that dart about nervously, scanning their surroundings for potential threats or problems. Some Sixes have said that they report being aware of where exits are in any room they are occupying and what stands between them and the exit. This can be very stressful and can shape their imaginations, resulting in a constant expectation of mishap or danger.

+ Sixes are suspicious of other people's motives.
+ Sixes can attribute motives to others that aren't true—what is that person thinking of me, probably something negative, fearing other people's feelings about them. They can be seen as paranoid to a certain extent.
+ They might join a like-minded group to avoid becoming paranoid.

Suspicion, procrastination, and searching for hidden motives can become useful tools—suspicion of authority can evolve into constructive critique, and procrastination can lead to allowing time for the reformulation and reevaluation of ideas. Imaging the worst can become believable enough to replace reality in a paranoid episode, but that same powerful imagination can generate original solutions.

Sixes are able to identify with underdog causes and are capable of loyal unrewarded effort for a cause or a creative ideal. They have capacities for great self-sacrifice in the name of duty or responsibility to others. Sixes are willing to go against the odds and against the status quo for a worthwhile venture, particularly if in collaboration with allies.

+ Hierarchical environments with clearly defined lines of authority and clearly defined problem areas are attractive to Sixes.

Acceptance

Sixes are always worrying about something. Their anxiety can be a great source of suffering for them. A doubting mind can drive a Six up the wall, along with others with whom the Six is interacting. Knowing that the Six suffers from their own minds and have a powerful imagination for seeing the worst-case scenarios in any situation leads us to a level of acceptance and compassion because we can understand and relate to their doubting selves, anxiety, and worrying. Just knowing that they go through this process on a daily basis of projecting their doubts and fears into their realities makes us feel like they suffer in a way which we can relate to. We've all had anxiety before and have doubts and fears, but the Six has these ongoing internally and suffers from their internal doubting selves on a regular basis as a way of life.

Perhaps your parent is a Six. You might come to understand that they adopt a role of being an authority through their role as a parent even when you are already grown up and an adult; thus, when the Six comes out as an authority, you now are able to recognize that the Six is identifying as a parental authority and isn't necessarily trying impose their way on their child but simply trying to keep things in order.

Also, because you now know that trust is a significant issue within a six, you can more easily give them what they crave—reassurance. When you give a Six reassurance about something, that person feels relieved. Further, growing and building trust with a Six is a great way of loving and accepting a Six into your life. That Six will learn to ask your opinion before making a decision. Thus, you become a confidant of that Six. Reassurance also helps the Six with his doubting mind. Easing doubts is another way of loving and accepting a six. If the issue of trust comes up, you will now be ready to show that you can be trusted.

If your child is a Six, you can guide that child into jobs and situations that give them structure as well as well-defined lines of authority and expectations. You can nurture your child's need to be prepared for dangers. You can simply be aware of their attitudes toward authority, whether it is the school principal, teachers, parents themselves, or police. That awareness is acceptance. You can frequently give Sixes reassurance and love them with the understanding that they experience anxiety and doubt often.

Do not judge the Six for his or her anxiety; instead, understand that it is a part of their personality structure. Reassurance that everything is okay is a better way to relate to their anxiety than to criticizing the Six for worrying, doubting, or not trusting something or someone. The Six can exhaust himself and others with constant worrying and watching for danger. Recognizing that this is part of how he is built can help you not get irritated or angry or down emotionally and rather proceed with the Six in a more open-minded way. The Enneagram gives us acceptance of Type and also helps us maintain an open mind and be less judging toward others.

CHAPTER 8

TYPE SEVEN

I LIKE TO CALL SEVEN THE dancing mind. Their minds are nimble and quick. They see many possibilities in any situation. My roommate in law school would comment on how he was seeing all kinds of possibilities in the football game we were watching, much more than the rest of us who were just watching the game without really analyzing it. The Seven's mind is anticipatory. Sevens foresee events and generate ideas on the fly, favoring activities that stimulate their minds and in turn generate more things to do and think about. They are gifted in brainstorming and synthesizing information. Their minds are always chattering. It sometimes seems as though they are thinking about ten things at once.

+   Ask the Seven about their minds being nimble and quick and if they frequently analyze the positive possibilities in any situation. They should identify with their minds being active in these ways.

Sevens are mental types that carry the party forward. They are like Peter Pans who celebrate with an imaginary feast at the dinner table. They celebrate with great enthusiasm and seek pleasure through the gathering of friends and excitement in any given situation. Sevens may come across as fun people. They get enthusiastic about having and seeking pleasure. They can be seen as enthusiastic about almost anything that catches their attention.

Sevens are the future thinkers; for them, the present is made tolerable by the future. Sevens always envision us moving in to a golden age. Things are going to get better. They, however, are not as deep thinkers as Fives. Instead, they see in a shallower way but at the same time with many possibilities presenting themselves.

- Sevens don't handle the bad with the good well. They fear being brought down emotionally and avoid being disheartened. They have a need to stay emotionally up.
- The passion of the Seven is gluttony. Not gluttony for food, necessarily, but gluttony for experience. When eating at a restaurant, the Seven prefers the buffet for its many positive edible parts rather than choosing one item from the menu. However, once the choice is made, there is often the letdown of noticing what wasn't chosen. Ask the prospective Seven if this example resonates with them.
- The Seven constantly seeks new and exciting experiences.
- They can have problems with superficiality and impulsiveness.
- One of the Seven's main problems is that he or she can get easily distracted and can get too scattered.

+ They approach life with curiosity, optimism, and a sense of adventure, much like a kid in a candy store who looks at the world in wide-eyed rapt anticipation of all the good things.

The Seven will identify with the above statements. See also if you can observe a Seven getting excited or enthusiastic about a new adventure. Perhaps the conversation is about where to go on a vacation—watch as his nimble mind analyzes all the possibilities in a quick way; watch as enthusiasm grows when analyzing the possibilities. Sevens can also be observed by their spontaneity and desire to live life fully with all the enjoyment of any and all possibilities.

+ Sevens like keeping options open.
+ They can't stand boredom and make sure they are never boring themselves.
+ Sevens are exhilarated by the rush of ideas and by the pleasure of being spontaneous, preferring broad overviews and the excitement of the initial stages of the creative process to probing a single topic in depth.

Sevens are extremely optimistic, exuberant, and upbeat. They are endowed with abundant vitality and a desire to fully participate in their lives each day. They are naturally cheerful and good-humored, not taking themselves or anything else too seriously. When they are balanced within themselves, their joy and enthusiasm for life naturally affects everyone around them. They remind us of the pure pleasure of existence.

- Sevens have a self-image of being happy, spontaneous, and outgoing.
- Sevens put few brakes on themselves and dislike boundaries or limitations of any kind. They want to be free to respond to impulses and desires as soon as they arise and without delay.
- A typical Seven philosophy is enjoy now, pay later. Sevens have a tendency to use money for exciting adventures; maybe too much money.
- They excel at considering options that others might not perceive.
- Sevens have a great ability to maintain a positive outlook and a sense of abundance.

The above statements are identifiers that can be used to ask questions of the Seven by rephrasing the statements into questions, as each chapter in this book is used that way.

Acceptance

Since Sevens have a need to be emotionally up to avoid feelings of emptiness inside, a level of acceptance generates when the Seven rejects dealing with the darker sides of life. You can understand that he needs to stay positive and emotionally up and therefore accept him when he has a hard time dealing with depressing or uncomfortable negative feelings and situations. Also, one can understand and accept when the Seven is acting like the life of the party when nobody else around him is feeling like they want to share his celebratory attitude. I was once at a dinner gathering where the Seven was carrying the party forward by reveling in the many options on the menu. However, everyone else was lamenting how much everything cost at this expensive restaurant. The Seven there couldn't understand why everyone was complaining and had a hard time with it.

Sevens aren't good with negative, darker emotions inside themselves and in others. They have difficulty acknowledging the pain that others experience. Knowing this creates acceptance that the Seven you are talking to isn't going to be good at understanding your depression. Maybe finding someone else to talk to would be better. Maybe you can select a different psychologist since the Seven psychologist you are seeing has a hard time dealing with the darker side of your depression.

Sevens bond over the possibilities in a situation. You can love a Seven by sharing his enthusiasm for what could happen in a positive way. For example, when planning a vacation, the Seven will revel in all the possibilities of where the family might go. His mind acts quickly and gets excited about all the ideas he can come up with. Going with the Seven mind and engaging him over his ideas will be giving to a Seven.

Sometimes, Sevens try multiple jobs or careers as a way of moving from one job that felt boring or started to lead to unpleasant feelings. Understanding the Seven's need not to feel bored and not to deal with the unpleasantness of a particular job can generate acceptance. Instead of challenging the Seven and blaming him for not succeeding at his career, one might relate to the Seven and understand that it is part of his personality type to move to another career.

Sevens have difficulty living in the present moment and instead gravitate toward planning and considering possibilities. The constant planning is enjoyable, but it leads to escapism and gluttony. They go from one idea to the next and keep anticipating possibilities for the future. This can lead to a great deal of stress because they can't focus and accomplish as much as they would like. Gluttony, the passion of the Seven, is an attachment to consumption; it is a need to be constantly taking something in, chewing and tasting rather than fully digesting anything. Gluttony is a way of handling their anxiety. When anxiety comes up and the Seven is not receiving stimuli from the outside world, an inner hunger arises behind that hunger pain and the feeling of being deprived of something arises. When Sevens feel this, their immediate reaction is to fill this gap with external experiences or something else that will make them happy. Understanding the Seven pattern of planning to avoid anxiety can lead to acceptance of this planning and analysis of possibilities.

One can love a Seven by helping them to enjoy the moment and not to plan out so much. Acceptance of their internal drive for possibility analysis, coupled with an attitude of trying to stay present in the moment, is engaging the Seven in a healthy way.

CHAPTER 9

TYPE EIGHT

THE EIGHT OFTEN FILLS THE ROLE of "boss" (a word that can describe the Eight personality). Eights are typically in positions of being the boss in order to stay in control. The boss role is usually seen in a work context, but it can also be engaged in within a family context. An Eight parent might take on a role similar to a boss. One eight said, "It just seems that's where I get stuck. Whether it is intentional or not, I don't know. I am very happy being the boss. I like having some control over my environment. To that degree, I like to dictate how my environment is going to be run."

- The core value of the Eight is fairness. Thus, the following question arises (remember to watch his energy, his identification with his response to the question, and whether he seems to say this from his heart as if fairness matters to him): What does the word "fairness" mean to you?

He might say that fairness is very important to me. He might nod his head at the question. He might talk about fairness as something he needs in his life.

+ Good follow-up questions to his response might be:
  Do you resolve conflicts you have with others by
  trying to get to a fair result? Is that a primary way
  you try to resolve conflicts or just once in a rare while?
  How much do you identify with fairness as being a
  part of your life? Ask for the Eight to give you an
  example of how fairness plays a role in his or her life.

One Eight told me the following, "I can't stand someone
else being treated unfairly. Whether my actions are fair is
a question for me. I conduct myself with that barometer of
fairness. It is highly important to me. I resolve conflicts with
others by using fairness. I identify very much so with fairness
being a part of my life." Clearly, her energy picked up, and
she had a lot to say, indicating she identified with fairness as
a core value.

The Eight can be observed by how physical his presence
feels to you. Eights are very physical people. They use body
language as a way to get around and communicate. See if you
can observe whether they are body-oriented people. If you
can narrow the person down to a body type because of the
way he or she expresses themselves—frequently using body
language and being physical in some way that they seem to
communicate or identify with that physicality—then you
are left with a decision of how to narrow down the potential
Eight to a One, Eight, or Nine. One Eight told me that he
got around Europe using body language rather than speaking
the language of the country he was in.

+ Eights think in terms of physicality and project that
  physicality into their environment.

Another way to observe whether a person is an Eight is by the way they project themselves in a room. They literally fill their environment up by speaking louder than everyone else or might act like a boss in front of others or in a group. This type doesn't hide itself. Rather, Eights are very present with others and manifest themselves as sometimes intimidating to others. If you can observe a potential Eight as being a bossy type of person and if they are projecting their sense of fairness onto the situation and trying to resolve a conflict with others by being aggressive, pushy, or overbearing, you have found the person to be an Eight.

Eights are not shy of conflict or confrontation. They like debate and don't shy away from a good engaging debate. They can come across as overly aggressive. In fact, the Eight enjoys a good fight and often engages in fights as a way of satisfying their passion—lust. Lusting is not easy to describe, but once you get the hang of it, it becomes easier to observe. Lust doesn't just mean sexually, but it also applies in terms of food, engaging their physicality, and entering into confrontation or for experience. Since the passion on the Enneagram manifests frequently, notice lust where you can. The Eight engages in more confrontational fighting styles of behavior because he feels more connected and alive when doing so. The passion of the Eights compels them to act in ways that stimulate feelings of aliveness, leading them to live intensely. Interactions with others must be intense, work must be intense, and play must be intense, as if Eights had to constantly push against life.

- Eights can be very goal-oriented and push others aside to get their goals accomplished.

- Eights seek to correct injustice. They vent their anger or discomfort at injustices that they see. They often overlap this with their core value of fairness—fairness is used as a legitimizing way of correcting injustice. In other words, they will try to make things fair when correcting injustices.

- Eights cannot stand to be used or manipulated. Eights don't want to be controlled or to allow others to have control over them, whether the power is psychological, sexual, social, or financial.

Making decisions for an Eight is not difficult; Eights do that with their gut. The gut tells them what to do.

- Self-reliance is important to an Eight.

- A fight is not a negative thing to an Eight. What you see as a fight or a potentially confrontational conversation could be seen as just a good debate to an Eight. One Eight said, "I don't like to pick fights, but I don't shy away from them."

- They can come across as powerful, dominating, willful, confrontational, and decisive. They have enormous willpower and vitality and feel most alive when they are exercising these capacities in the world.

- Eights are rugged individualists. More than any type, they stand alone. They want to be independent and resist being indebted to anyone.

- Eights can have a resourceful can-do attitude as well as a steady inner drive. They take the initiative and make things happen with a great passion for life. They are honorable and authoritative, natural leaders who have a solid, commanding presence. Their grounded-ness gives them abundant common sense as well as the ability to be decisive. Eights are willing to take the heat, knowing that any decision cannot please everyone.

Eights can be guarded about their feelings.

+ Like being tough to get their way, Eights believe they need to be tough and fight for everything they have or they'll be eaten alive.

+ Some Eights see themselves as the rock, the strong and impregnable one, the foundation for others in their family or professional circle. "I'm tough—I'm the one everyone else has to depend on." Ask prospective Eights if they identify with this mentality.

+ Eights like straight talk; they have difficulty understanding why others are not as forthright as they are. At the same time, some other types are confounded by how audacious and forceful Eights can be.

+ Eights need clear boundaries; they want to know where they stand with others as well as where they end and where others begin. They want to know what others will tolerate and what they will not. Eights discover boundaries by testing them. Eights will continue to push for boundaries until they get a reaction.

+ "My way or the highway—do it because I said so!" can be a reaction from an Eight at times.

+ Honor may be an important trait to Eights. Their word is their bond. When they say that you have their word on something, they mean it.

+ Courageous and strong but gentle and humble, Eights are willing to put themselves in jeopardy for the sake of justice and fairness.

Acceptance

Eights sometimes come across as intimidating and confrontational. But to them, they are just finding connection and acting out their lust. Acceptance of this type is easy. Engage them in the same way that they are engaging with you. Be confrontational back, use body language to match theirs, and hash out the fight with them. They will only appreciate it and not feel as though you are being too intimidating. Loving and accepting an Eight is to be straightforward. Be open and willing to get into a discussion on fairness. Again, matching the Eight on where he is coming from is a good way of developing understanding and acceptance of the Eight. Be loud back. Be assertive. Be open to being confrontational back at them, and they will feel like you are just relating to them in a constructive way.

Acceptance of the Eight passion for lust is also a good way to understand and therefore accept the Eight. They lust after food, for example. They might be seen as eating a lot and reveling in the food in a certain way. Even the way Eights engage with others is a manifestation of their lust. They are lusting after experiences; thus, the Eight can be very engaging in a conversation even though they might come across as confrontational and intimidating. Eights think of themselves as straightforward people; they don't hide from anything. Understanding these points about Eights can lead to an extremely positive level of awareness.

CHAPTER 10

TYPE NINE

N INES HAVE BEEN CALLED THE PEACEMAKERS because they see all sides of other people's positions and perspectives well and have a natural ability to find compromise and listen well to others.

- Nines are afraid of conflict and their own anger. They repress their anger and try to avoid conflicts. Ask the potential Nine if this is the case. Conflict is uncomfortable for Nines; they avoid it at all costs. "I just listened. I didn't voice my opinion."

- Nines tend to bottle up their anger, meaning that they suppress their anger. Then, seemingly out of the blue, they explode in anger at someone or something. That is a typical trait of type Nine. Ask the Nine if he has the experience of not getting angry for a long time and then blowing up at someone he felt angry toward but didn't constructively express discontent with prior to the outburst of anger. One Nine said, "The cumulative effect of these smaller things blew up to be something major."

+ Unlike an Eight or possibly a One, the Nine will never confront someone face-to-face in an extremely critical manner.

Nines have a passion of sloth or indolence, also called self-forgetting. They would rather zone out and just be than work to accomplish goals. The metaphor of the couch potato describes a Nine's style of avoidance.

+ Ask prospective Nines if they have a habit of sloth, indolence, or self-forgetting. The passion of Nines causes them to distract themselves from their problems by consuming food, using drugs, watching television, or oversleeping. If any of these resonate with the person you are trying to type, you have determined them to be a Nine. Sloth comprises part of the passion of the Nine personality type. It is hard to motivate, easy to procrastinate, and comfortable to engage in self-forgetting activities.

One Nine I spoke with went bug-eyed when I mentioned the word "sloth." I was able to type her based on that reaction alone. This is an example of how someone's reactions or responses to questions are something he or she identifies with. The bug-eyed reaction was an identifier of herself as understanding that she has sloth as part of her personality type.

Nines are good at listening to other people's positions and merging with them so as to see all sides of an issue. Rather than assert their own perspective, they merge with others' perspectives in order to resolve an issue. Because they are so attuned through their fixation of attention to other people's positions, they tend to not know their own opinions. At the Enneagram intensive workshop I attended in 2001, the Nines were the last to finish a self-awareness exercise because they were altogether busy listening to each other's positions rather than having to assert one dominant way of responding to the exercise. They took a long time because everyone's opinion seemed reasonable to them. Ask the Nine whether they have a harder time asserting their opinion in a group.

Nines are excellent at understanding other people. Their fixation of attention is to merge with another person's heart and feel the other person's feelings to be a part of their own. That leads to both an intuitive understanding of others as well as a difficulty with understanding their own feelings.

+ Nines need to feel comfortable in every sense of the word.

+ Nines have a materialistic streak. It is hard for them to not want to possess more stuff such as clothing.

+ Nines are excellent mediators; they have a natural ability to see everyone's point of view.

+ Nines have an ability to co-process information such as having the TV on, listening to the washing machine in the background, and talking on the phone all at once and still assimilating all that is going on around them. This is a natural ability of the Nine.

+ Nines can be described as receptive, reassuring, agreeable, and complacent.

+ A good strength of type Nine is a profound patience and a deep letting be of other people that allows others to develop in their own way, such as a parent who patiently teaches his or her children new skills while remaining at a respectful but watchful distance. "I do think I'm good at letting people develop in their own way and give them space and not pushing them to be different," one Nine told me.

Nines are good at including others.

+ Nines shun calling personal attention to themselves; they place others before themselves and have a hard time being primary in their own and other people's attention. They prefer to give others the limelight. Rarely asserting themselves, they like keeping things harmonious and pleasant and have difficulty doing or saying anything that others might find offensive, uncomfortable, or controversial

+ In a relationship with others, the Nine often gives up his or her own agenda in favor of the other person's.

+ Nines often feel as though they don't know where they get their information from, but all believe it to be correct information.

+ When going on vacation, unlike the Three, the Nine would rather do nothing and relax than keep busy and active.

+ Nines can be very sensitive to criticism. They overly accept criticism from others. It is difficult for them to not merge with the opinions of others, making it hard to reject criticism they disagree with. They may care too much about what others think of them.

+ Nines can have difficulty figuring out what they want; they can get confused by what is the best course of action for themselves.

◆ Nines fear not being listened to and often think others are not listening to them. They want to be taken seriously and feel as if others are ignoring them.

Acceptance

Understanding that the Nine has a passion of sloth creates acceptance that they have difficulty at first getting motivated and into action. It is hard not to procrastinate when sloth kicks in. Understanding that the Nine has a hard time getting off the couch and into action is a compassionate way of understanding that they have a hard time with accomplishing tasks.

Further, Nines need to be comfortable. A friend who is a Nine told me she felt herself needing comfort—food wise, survival wise, financially, and even the specific type and nature of her mattress had to be comfortable in a certain way for her to sleep at night.

Not wanting to be in the limelight and having a hard time speaking up in class and voicing their opinions is a hard area for the Nine at times. Recognizing this is accepting them for their weaknesses. They would rather be in the background than the focus of everyone's attention. Further, acceptance of Nines means recognizing their great ability to see others' points of view. This is an asset to them.

As a Five myself, I've wrestled with my own desire to be a minimalist and not collect stuff with my type Nine sister's desire to collect stuff and material things. Accepting her as a Nine and understanding my own dislike of collecting too many things gives me the ability to choose to go her way and let her buy as many books she wants instead of insisting that we buy only one or two because of my own minimalism.

Knowing that Nines are sensitive to criticism and take criticism to heart too much can enable you to couch your criticism in softer language and put it in a constructive way. You can also tell the Nine that you aren't criticizing him in a negative way. Giving the Nine positive feedback in a giving, positive way can go a long distance for a Nine who takes others' opinions to heart too much. They may feel relief when receiving positive feedback after performing or for some task they accomplished.

Just knowing about the different Enneagram personality types and correctly figuring out people's Enneagram types leads to acceptance. All of the above is meant to stimulate your understanding of the things different Enneagram types identify with.

CHAPTER 11

DOING A TYPING INTERVIEW

ONDUCTING A PROPER TYPING INTERVIEW JUST means sitting down with someone and asking questions based on the identifiers in each of the chapters about type. It means going through each of the nine chapters and asking questions such as, "Do you identify with having a strong inner critic?" Follow the responses with a follow-up question such as, "Do you feel like your inner critic criticizes you often?" (type One). Or, "Do you believe you are great at bargain hunting and often seek out bargains, discounts, and try to negotiate over a purchase's price?" (type Two). Based on the interviewee's responses, you can decide to ask more type One identification questions or choose to move on to another type. I suggest that while going through the identifiers in this book, you also keep watch for characteristics to observe. You should combine your questions with observations about the person you are interviewing. For example, pay attention to when the interviewee's energy picks up, where his or her excitement grows, and whether he laughs and agrees wholeheartedly with one of your questions. See if you can determine which identifiers the interviewee identifies with more than others. At the end of the interview, it is likely that your interviewee will want to know how you came to your conclusion. You can reiterate your understanding about type from this book and the identifiers, and you can see if you can tell the person what you observed about his or her behavior or energy during the interview.

A good place to start the interview is to ask the interviewee whether he feels like a mentally oriented person, a feeling-oriented person, or a physically oriented person. If the person knows himself enough, his response might guide you to one of three possibilities. A body/physical type would be One, Eight, or Nine; a feeling-oriented type would be Two, Three, or Four; and a mental type would be Five, Six, or Seven. You might then start with the body types if the person says they are physically oriented. Sometimes, making comparative statements is helpful in this regard. For example, ask, "Do you feel you are more mentally than feeling-oriented?" That can help you narrow down the possibilities more. The trick you will find, as I have, is that people don't really know even whether they are feeling- or mentally oriented. Sometimes, it is clear, but other times, it is not. They don't generally think about this topic and haven't done much self-awareness work before. That means their response could be misleading. But not to worry—that's why we have several questions and identifiers in this book for you to probe the interviewee further.

Ask if the interviewee feels he or she identifies with a statement in the chapters above, especially a bullet-pointed identifier. For example, ask potential Sevens if they identify with the statement that Sevens have dancing minds and frequently analyze many possibilities in any given situation. Just go down the list of statements, going from one type to the next. As you go through the nine types, pay attention to what comes up and follow accordingly. Remember that you may need to ask the prospective types whether they would identify with the statements in this book during their twenties or thirties. The grip of the Enneagram Personality Type is stronger in those time periods. You can bring this point up multiple times during your typing interview. Was your inner critic stronger in your twenties or thirties? (An example for a One). Did you adjust your image to look more successful in your twenties or thirties? (An example for a Three).

You don't need to go in any particular order through the Enneagram. I like to start with asking type One questions based on identifiers and simply go through the numbers in sequence. If you start to figure out that the person is a feeling-oriented person, say you observe him being emotive, emotional, or outwardly expressing feelings and then try going immediately to types Two, Three, or Four.

Another point to raise is that the Enneagram types are about a person's insides. It is a description of inner behavior that is frequently manifesting within us. Try to remember that the identifiers in this book are something that happen inside the type and are experienced on a daily basis. For example, asking a prospective type whether he has a doubting mind may lead him to say that he does since he has doubts about something going on at work. But that isn't the Enneagram Six's doubting mind. Rather, it is just having doubts about one issue. The Six has a doubting mind that happens every day and isn't just more isolated to a particular moment or to a one-time experience of doubting something going on at work. Thus, when doing an interview, it can be helpful to ask if a potential Six, for example, has worry, doubt, and anxieties daily or frequently. When a person answers "sometimes" to a question you ask them, you might follow with a question about how frequently that doubt, worry, or anxiety manifests inside them. Do that to distinguish whether the doubting is a part of their type or just part of being human. We all have doubts as human beings, but it is the doubting mind of the Six that sets him apart from other types and manifests daily as part of their Six suffering.

Doing an interview is a solid way of learning the type of others.

Learning to Follow

Part of learning how to do an interview is learning the concept of following. Following means carrying a conversation forward. People like to talk about things when they matter to their hearts. It feels good to be followed. The reason for you to follow someone is to bring her out and to see more clearly whether she identifies as the particular type you are asking questions about. If the person you are asking questions of and trying to figure out the personality type of seems to identify with one of the identifiers or statements in this book, then you should follow that person on that particular topic. When you notice someone's energy pick up, that is when you want to follow him. The reason we follow is to dig deeper into what they are feeling when they identify with a statement or question. You can ask, as a way of following, for the prospective type to give you an example of what they are saying. You can also ask if they identify with that statement and whether they can comment further. Another way to follow is to express a feeling on the topic that the prospective type is talking about. For example, a person may identify with and get more animated about the topic of privacy. You should follow up with even something as basic as "Oh, that's interesting—can you tell me more about that?"; "Can you give me an example?"; "Do you identify with privacy being important to you?" "How important?" Maybe you'll express a feeling to follow such as, "I am also a private person and value my privacy more than most of my friends." Encouraging a person to comment is following them. Once you learn to bring a person's heart out, you are on the path to determining their Enneagram type.

CONCLUSION

A GOOD WAY TO PRACTICE YOUR typing skills is to ask these questions and observe these subjects of a person you already know to be a certain type. That way, you will be able to detect with more certainty how the type comes out and how to understand what the type identifies with.

Over the years, I have discussed the Enneagram with many people. Everyone seems to resonate to a certain extent with their type. Not everyone, however, is aware of his or her type because much of it is unconscious or subconscious. As you use this book to bring out type-based identifications, remember that much of the material may be something that is recognized only some of the time. "Sometimes," a One said to me in response to all of my questions for her. That is still an identification. Following the "sometimes" response with a question such as, "Does this happen to you on a daily basis?" or "Was this stronger for you in your twenties and thirties?" can be helpful in developing more of an identification with type. The truth is that the type is almost always in operation. It is constantly manifesting itself inside us. That is why the Enneagram is so powerful as a map of our insides. You just need to make things a little bit more conscious and start to inwardly observe what is going on to start to figure out the contours of your or others' Enneagram types.

My aim in writing this book is to give you the ability to both observe type through telltale signs as well as observe what the prospective types identify with through questions or an interview. Following observation comes interviews or just questions to ask about the different types. Once you've identified the type, acceptance follows. With acceptance comes understanding and compassion, and that acceptance and compassion are often a form of love. Good luck on your Enneagram journey through life. I wish you all the most success in typing others.

About the Author

Josen Kalra was born in upstate New York. His parents are from the northern state of Punjab in India. He grew up mostly in Southern California and attended University of California, Berkeley as an undergraduate. Following his graduation at the University of California, Berkeley, he travelled through Central America and then Nepal, India, and Thailand. He then attended Columbia Law School and graduated from there in 2002. He worked as an attorney for a few years and found that his passion was writing. He started his own freelance writing business in 2011. Josen loves writing, chess, and traveling. His family, two parents and a younger sister, are his support and strength. Josen also enjoys teaching others through writing and looks forward to engaging anyone in a conversation about self-awareness and the Enneagram.

Printed in the United States
By Bookmasters